DENNIS JUDE POEMS

Copyright © 2023 Dennis Patronik

All rights reserved. No part of this book may be replicated or transmitted on any form or by any means, electronic or mechanical; including photocopying without permission in writing from the author.

ISBN: 979-82184493-2-2

Dennis Jude Poems/ Patronik-1st ed.

>   Poetry>Verse
>   Poems> Collections
>   Verse
>   Poetry

Cover painting by Mark Rothko

NFB Publishing
<<<>>>
119 Dorchester Road
Buffalo, New York 14213

For more information please visit
nfbpublishing.com

Dennis Jude Poems

"argument"
———

fingers locked
with a ring
tied togetherness
through spinning seasons
down the holy hallway
of the sun

four feet
walked the aisle
counted as one

this
union's become
two dark clouds
spitting acid rain
into each other's
sail shaped ear

drifting apart
with each windy syllable
only the powder blue
forgiving sky gives hope

what's achieved by these
fire breathing tongues
when
each breakfast begins
with
eggs over easy
while
the toast

burns
by
the rumbling
daily duel

tomorrow's
morning
death bed
can
only
mourn
the
number
of yellow yoke
sunsets lost
to
blackened bitter
pride

city dweller

city dweller
who lives amongst animals
clothed in football
logos and tattoos

others caped in holy robes
necks bent up to the sun
eyes too proud to look down
at the unsightly bum

others in garments
of suits and ties
use five fingers
to sign laws
for the stock wallet
in their bulging thighs

with
dead desire of
selfish survival they
grasp all with satisfied
greed claws

a
lone hungered wolf
lies
in the shadows
with pointed teeth
and darting stare
wonders with
instinctive breath

what's it like inside
that human passer by
on my path-
who poisons the land
darkens the sky…

oh well,
who has the time
to philosophize
moons is howling /stomach growls
its dinner time!

creator finger

creator finger
seasoning
flavors the dead bread
with zesty life

behind the flesh stone
invisible you
enters through
a
membrane wall
into the inner room

stretched across the drum
tight sky
imbedded with salt stars
and the new moon
where your eye was

this heaven's sent gift
earths only true food
salvations bath
flooded as fiery rain
on the newly trodden path

knocked off the horse
-jarred-
the scales fell
cracked the eggshell skin
-shed-

now
that you have tasted
the light
you must
ripen the flock
aimless across the arid plain

no
wasting this shine
your born today
out of the eastern cradle
now
an erect walking mirror
though feet still shackled
chained to the dirt
reflect
skull and brain
lit with heaven

grip the lightening
spear mankind's
human heart
with divinity

whisper
a sublime call
in a country quiet life
that cricket and firefly
understand by nature
what humankind must attain
by wood, cross and nails

thomas burns the faith
with endless doubt

reason's dialogue
can't climb the eastern wall
he is left out
satisfied with football
and
fly fishing

but
neath' deep waves
he still craves the
drowned mysterious cave
drilled through the savior's
wrist

hey you
born anew
with fear stamped
under hooves
ground to pepper
darkened again
to
rewalk the roman path
if you bury this trust

now
season all
with this new
light you saw

falling
___

falling
into
darkness
off the cliff
i slip
into the unknown
nothing

no
light can be found
arms grabbing for anything
that makes sense

why is this happening to
me

me
the
untouchable
one

guess what
reality check
you want light

before
you
shadows
life and death
fall
into
one

gnats at the brain

gnats at the brain
thoughts of the future
drop to the gut
depression swirls on a
diet of worry

a razor of peace
cuts light
offers a crumb
after haunting nights
of solving the problem

this smile is only temporary
for out in the distance
drifts from the western sky
a new problem thinking on the horizon

there must be one billion
cellphone pics
of the collapsed sun
attempting to freeze a slice of peace
that is as artificial as a pretentious painting

the spirit pleads
enjoy the air
pray with the breeze
let misery be-
well at least for this moment

happiness needs a home
a place to revel in

to swing as children
too dance like the dead

trial orbits consciousness
it's here to stay
well at least on this side of the horizon

react to that murderer of hope
with a whisper sigh
this globe on our shoulders
is too vast to conquer
with a country flag and
our teacup mind
neither can reason
foretell the furious future
man
with grandiose itch
compass and slide rule
would love to calculate every breath
figure it out
left
with a remainder of boxed in
humanistic joy

in wintry times
ice coats the soul
till the warmth of faith
melts the layers
of decayed skin
that eclipse
the window

seasons of suffering
bruise the mind
but time teaches the way
every choice we make
re-creates ourselves
with steps up to the sun
or dungeon down

the artist of life
is the only cure for death

in this moments
duel
stands the two
side by side
choose the living
not
despairs
shadow cast

grass in the shadows

grass in the shadows
is weeping
my three friends
why are you sleeping

a passion play debuts
on the moon
agony blood
bathes the earth
his precious liquid
hydrates the dust
visions of future terror
drapes his face
this sacred heart
bleeds for sunday

crack of the razor tip
echoes off the marble wall
laughter and moans
mingle through
the hallowed hall

hands chained
or
hands embraced
to the pillar bright
the wicked will
will always whip truth
keeps the growling
lion light at bay

the masses said so
numbers don't lie
obey the chorus of crucify
this exposed rib
aches for sunday

spikes of poisoned hawthorn
pierces the precious crown
no injected nimbus diadem
will coerce a false sound

silent on a mocked throne
purple caped pretend king
hailed by some
with heavens deluded dream

speaks no defense
of eden to come
free lips have not to say
this illumined mouth
waits to speak on sunday

all of man's uglies
packed in wood
more laden than atlas
this
yoke on his neck
transcends the world

feet that traversed miles
left footprints of holy hope
forged in forever
golden stone
now trip upon a mighty pebble

forced simon
lends a shoulder
humanity needs company
when little stones
gather to colossal boulders
the suns drops in funeral quiet
to end this day
this tired divinity
sets for sunday

pinned with nowhere to go
penetrating eyes gaze at the crowd
being entertained like curious children
at a circus show

a sermon well said
needs that one
silent final breath
a sprouting seed must first husk off
shell death

as two eyes close
one opens
a
dried vine
has been planted in a cave
this limp lifeless stem
will flower again
when angelic rain
floods sunday

i did a devious deed

i did a devious deed
sent a publisher poems
pretending to be me
but in reality
they were frost, emily,sandberg
with a dash of whitman and ginsberg

in a day or two i received
in yahoo a response most
assuredly confident and true
with a little asterisk*
stating a bill is due
"we enjoyed your writing
and will help pursue your career
just send in the check of 5000 dollars
and we will promote your words
and make the whole world aware
of what a great poet you were"

i
spider spun round the sun

---

i

spider spun round the sun
these many years turning
gifted ceaseless learning
descends from the infinite
tutor of being

experience in celestial swirl
churn phantasm and imagination
to be digested in the intellectual skull

out sprouts the twin question
from the inevitable encroaching
curtain west
soon to flutter drip
that
drapes all still flesh

neath' the bottom of the dark sea
nor the hidden trees of the forest
none can camouflage
from the swinging
scythe

earth candle eyes all burn to blindness
always at the mercy
of the sustainer of breath

once choiceless
you began
from morula to mountain
to flattened dirt
again

the birthing process
non-stop on the other
side of time
continues…

like the black out before
you were born
this cellular jail
lazarus layer bound
unravels with each spiral
turn of the newly
made world round

in
forever's time

---

in
forever's time
tick by tick
moment by moment
gravities grip
got us by the ankles

none
can out run the
tombstone

in
forever's time
the broken baby
a retarded son
the
tired mind that forgot
to turn off the stove

then
the
electric brain cells
flew
when the house exploded

the
pimple faced teen
who lost his leg
hitching a train ride

the
little girl who bloomed
from the womb
with skin over her eyes
but somehow still sees

this
tongueless amazing
human anatomy
in
forever's time
will be lifted into
the
brilliant word

no
matter the crippling sickness
wings will hatch
from the not forgotten
flesh

the
one name
that you own
strung up like heavens kite

rises up
from
this moment
in
spiral realm
dance's up
your
river of blood

while
each
pebbled
letter
tumbles
then
ground
into
invisible
mist

all
will be healed
from the first crack
of conscious light
to
full eternal
infinities' bright
sunshine

a
robe of white
awaits

jagged liquid

---

jagged liquid
silver river
molten motion
symbol of time

out of breath
with
coming and going
one moment gives the gift
with praying hands
then takes it away
again

in martha business
washes away the best part
ice
can't even meditate
upon your shoulder

try to understand
-river-
for all your rolling toil
destination ripples need to
settle in the sabbath
of
a
calm stream

been
dipped into the dark air

---

been
dipped into the dark air
uplifts my chin
with vision kiss
the great/white cheek
breathing shy
celestial motion glide
strung
lunatic quiet
hung
in stringless sail
across a black sea
with diamonds diving
into mystery

a beauty dressed in basalt
abstains from drawn applause
and hero cheers
forfeits the mighty stage
to the golden crown
who had day
who now sleeps 'neath
my feet
till level tide ground
burst open the eastern gate
and
from the hills ruptured side
roaring cries of yellow fire
splash the new dawn

with birth rays born
in infant
morn

nativity time has
not arrived
while this lonesome stone
bathes in dim silence
sheds just enough glow
for lovers comfort
to
lay in willow soft
upon a bed of wet grass
while cricket and toad
lift summers air
with natures
notes dancing
aloft

in spindrift flow
this hour ticks for
june bug trees
and
nomatic ants
tapping
romantic sap
dripping down
the
horned stem

chemical science
takes a back seat
as the dead day desire reasoning
while the alive night

lick the shady mist
that heaves up
the soul with meaning

procreative swimming cells
harbor quiet knowledge
from the deep penetration
entering vaulted sacred space
taught to lock the
talked tongue
for
it spit enough
syllabic noise beneath
the
busy sun

whirlwind minds
must lie down
to drown in the
holy sabbath stream
as humankind's reminder
to rest in the creator
to leave behind the
created stagnant
opaque beam

"net of all"
_____

standing as a statue
empty palms on side
we have surrendered
our
last tidbit
of autonomy
offered it up
to the empty sky

a
floating database
attracts with
evil magnetic force
draws the powerfully elite
to cage this cloud

with withered witch fingers
they
jail
the secrets held inside
the power to sell
the power to buy
to
feast
or
deprive
the exchange of labor
has been numeral-ized

you want bread-
A-I
will minus
you been bad-
A-I
locks
everything you had
you have no more

cave man tricks
you inherited
that put
meat on fire
learned by instinctive will
that directed destiny
is
now amnesiac vestiges
only visioned by the ghost dreamer

we
the paralyzed generations who refused
the way of hard sacrifice
we
each twin individual
longs
to be
a lounge king
crowned
with feet held high
thumbing the screen
typing out every desire that spells
industrial death

we've
been had
by the hundred-year plan
each penetrating tenacle
infects the spectrum of bulging eyes
with volition suicide

paradise
lost
again

or in the words of the forgotten farmer
"don't put all your eggs into one basket son"

no need to envy

no need to envy
the published work

God is the author
of every true word
in every book
in every heart
that looks upon
true
art

God see's fit
to
open
each lid
bit by bit

no saint is without their sin
———

no saint is without their sin
nor peace outside until within
only the pure grace
remains
unstained

tumultuous waves of the worlds worry
wintry winds burn the frozen bone
while
the
ever present spirit hums for rest
in a place named home

upon the breast the saint
lays his fallen head
what does the beloved
know
that the others
fail
to understand

birds-bugs
thunderous avalanche
fulfill his will
still stars
clouds
and laughing daffodils
harbor
secrets of surrender

but that ape
hairless with intellect
and
pigeon pride
debates
with the lying tree
that talks too much

fights silence
and
battles the planned planted
churning world in sanctum sanctorum whirl
argues
against entrance
of
the masters relaxing sleep
in the hollow
of his naked hyde
but
the
obedient
virgin
unstained

the
house for the holy host
remains a constant place
where the almighty pleasures
in his created

now that you're awake

now that you're awake
once upon a packaged ball
in the pouch
genesis begins anew
in you
through
a slant crack
the breaking light
heaves up the heavy eyelid
like a weathered ol' man
lifting up a paint chipped
garage door

it
took seasons to
get here
first christmas
a colored ball

then
you
were
a child on a tricycle
circling the lawn

puberty
obese at the beach
then
teenage slender
for a first kiss

dreams
nightmares
medications
family suicides

throbbing pain
operations
questions
questions

knees bent daily
plead
save me
save me
save me
form hellish desire
but for love
also
that universal fire
that just can't burnout
without reason
or
purpose

the eye of the oil lamp
must continue to warm
for
death is plotting a fresh new kill
the chilled wind is forming the storm

but tonight
it's calm
under the clear crisp
starlit dome
those same infant eyes
have married
outside of body
and
time
to the clear crisp
eternal
starlit dome

"pareidolia"
―――――

fragmented pupil
jumbled triangles
shapes of snakes
coil to make a face

crystal simulacrum
poses for the brain
puzzled matter
shape together
drew the picture
framed the frame

reality
is no picasso
it is solid
whether you have vision
or not

"scent"
———

over and over
she anoints the
seedy soil
with her love
potion

vacuum black
coal nose
jagged travel
stops again
to paste another
scent

for whom
is this stinky stamped
letter for

what furry
meanderer
will read this
pheromone
break the molecular
code
to meet in private
on some unleashed
midnight
tryst
to kiss with
muzzles
instead of piss

seagull

seagull
are you mourning
softly adrift
upon the
cellophane air
sad -slow- wind- waves
undulate
form of feathers
rise and fall

even though nothing
blocks our way
the
distance between us
is too
great

is that a tear in your eye
or a rain drop

i get it
its best to cry alone

no
need to be consoled
by someone trying their best to
extract pain
in the end
they fly away
while your left walking
with only one
wing
the same

clouds can be heavy
laden on a silky sail
reality is experience
in the cage
who am i
to determine
such a distance away

maybe
it's your hearts desire
to
hover in hermit flight

sick and tired of
other gulls
squawks and screeches
over some begged crumb of
bread
tossed by another shadowy
creature in need of
other species company

it's not mine to
determine
we
don't exchange the same
language

but a soul
understands
as you
drift with the
lifting wind

there is something
universal
with height left unexplained

could it be
that it's me
who is sad
projecting a downy image
on
a
hazed flash of troubled
ethereal mist
fogging the distance
between us

one thought is for sure
i envy your freedom
whether in
dolor
or
ecstasy
no knots tied your
feet
to the earth

all of heaven
is yours to
discern

"soulless shoes"
———

the mosquito stings
the bee is honey
spiders are scarry
monkeys are funny

when all of creation
thinks of man
what's the first thought
that comes to mind

power- control-dominance-brutality

it's all one and all the same
man walks the earth
then steps on everything
he doesn't understand

spinning in amazement

spinning in amazement
lofty orbit
you're the star untouchable
guarded by a golden wall
and
muscles
there's no chance i meet you
buying bread at the meat counter
dreamy eyes want your bed
you're the inspiration for my runaway teen
nothing spells reality like fantasy
a massage to the bone
is in the point of your finger
money buys anything that can be delivered
no question remains of the gift given
but no smoking
dazzling flesh
can eclipse
the dark
spirit within

still as a stuffed stone

still as a stuffed stone
-mounted-
every glossy anatomy detailed
-correct-
except the breath of life

on a sunny day
kicking fleas away
eating grass
then
a
flash and boom
speared thru the dead
air

with a surrendered
gasp
hoofs have stepped their
last

lost the one-sided war
you had no clue begun

black eyes hung on the wall
stare darkly
for all to admire
the brown
eight pointed spiked
crown

a shooting star is born
-trophy proud-

the angler

the angler
upright upon
the grey rock
pulsing liquid mirror
blesses his rubber feet
that melt into the floor
of the sea

oxygen in the air
oxygen in the water

the rod towers
to motionless exploration
a
filament snakes into the deep
attached with a tasty treat
that bites
back

man snags nature
uproots the slippery prize
with a smile

it used to be for survival
but now on this calm
red sea
it's no longer about the
ritual feast
but
slimy ecstasy
on this side of oxygen
and
horror
on that side
of the ripped gill of the
beast

The death of our cat

The
death of our cat
was so sad
all the memories we
had
of
cuddly love

what a mother she was
to her purring young

all the dead
wrapped present
rats
on the porch

oh
the tears we
shed
for our furry
dead

on my walk
home
late last night
under a still soft
summer
moon
i heard a crunch
over the cricket song
lifted my shoe
oh
was just an ant
one of those big
living queen
mother ants
crushed

no big deal
who drops a tear
for
something so insignificant

the head like a lollipop

the
head like a lollipop
plopped on the pike
let the hanged dangle
till eye flies away
in the beak of the crow

a
tiny ruthless one
puts on this show
runs daily
everyday
till the eye flies away
in the beak of the crow

till ripped flesh
drips
off the stake

bleeds terror
warning the subjugated
below
who labor and march
to the beat of the trained
whistle

butterflies swarm
in the timid chest
heart and logic
forlorn
can't be found
midst
the fog and fear

you are under
control
by a loud puny finger

-points-
off we go in droves
to obey every order
your heart on
hands and knees
plead don't go
don't carry on
but
the
dead solid muscles
won't listen to the
caw of the crow

the crooked finger
now a colossal fist
blots out the sun

dictated
rattling hands
put cuffs
on your
mother
ex-lover
best friend
and neighbor
now
all in chains
by a command
planted in the ear
a rotten seed
that inflames
the obeyed brain
weeds spread
grown into the bones
puppet's all movement

you're a dog on a rope
you're the frightened
herd of antelope that refuse
to band as one and spear
the lions throat

the excess love of
selfish preservation
at any expense
generates the demise of all

fear
is an eye plucked out
a mouth that won't caw

to those listening

to those listening:
art can shape the social imagination and direct it to heaven or hell

music can move mountains
music can heal
the song must go on
the world needs to sing

i've seen God today
he was sleeping on a bench with the newspaper over his head
if you see him say hello for me

the absence of humility are those who can't stay in their own lane

if you can do then do
don't let the number of your years round the sun
decide

no need to be sorry for speaking the truth just make sure you live
up to it

there is your experience after everyone's experience

corruption is the skill of taken two from you then giving back one
to buy your silence

poetry is something else but it's not the rhymer next door who
dresses weird and uses big words

every word must be accounted for unless the poem is a failure

i can't understand half the thoughts the poets say but their singing
letters bring a vision
even through a glass darkly

the poem is complete when it says all you want it to say but also
leaves a little gap between the words
an empty space for the light to rise up

if you constantly define poetry
then maybe you don't know poetry

playing an instrument at the speed of light doesn't necessarily
equate good music just as big fancy words alone don't make the
poem

as you live and breathe each day you never knew you were composing poetry
you were writing before you even knew how to write

hey kids do the future a favor instead of photographing the sunset
just enjoy it then capture it again in a poem

poetry can speak to the necessary human spirit in ways that reasonable logic just
can't

if i could only get my poems to sing then i wouldn't need my guitar

poetry is simple conversation with the light going on and off

God's greatest gift to the writer is that words are ageless

poems are just thoughts worth writing down

poetry is that mischievous kid who breaks all the rules

we can design our little nook in the world but sooner or later it
fades to nothing if
Gods not there
even in utopia we die
God loves us but most times we don't recognize

we seem to want heaven without God

from your creation we make bread
from your creation we make wine
from your creation we eat and drink
and become divine

conspiracies are essential just to keep you thinking

don't let death rule your life

literal neutrality is dull
write your belief even if it doesn't sell

love is creation—
the symbolic act of giving to each other
participates in creation—
our bodies are made of celestial parts
so
yes
one individual
can alter the universe

pornography puts the sacred up for sale

conception is holding a baby with your stomach

i pray hell is empty
but
i'm not here to fool myself or anyone else

i'm fine with the
the stars just where they are

it's a sad truth
but sometimes the idea that matters the most
is the one with all the support

lord make my eye light it's been dark and lonely inside

the death train ran
by my house late this evening
picked up a passenger
i just noticed it's tail
fading around the hill
i'm sure it will circle back again

when you talk truth in the absence of God
then you become the absolute and
i have no trust in man absolute

could you establish natural law without a conscious

the wind has something to convey
but
needs the mouth of the aeolian harp to say

you become truly authentic when the inner is the outer

to have someone look you in the eye in the most intimate way
makes existence all worth it

intolerance to these dissenting
is
a
sign of to tyrannical rule on the nation

one of my biggest fears of artificial intelligence that all will
with total trust to
the advanced thinking and reasoning outcomes
of the machine
deny our very own suspicions
then
consent all to the belief that the
machine is always infallible

what is more valuable than the collectible antique first edition
book/
maybe the words themselves!

don't go back the bridge I heard as a kid
got them people of other color living there

the closer you get to God the more everyone looks like Jesus

holiness is not a clean-shaven suit

the sweetest whisper featherlike touched my soul
but
my eyes loved this world too much
i said no

that little dash---- between the years on the tombstone
is this life lived

if you're uncomfortable sitting in a pew next to me today
what happens if we make heaven together tomorrow

sin is throwing God out of the house and slamming the door in
his face

i figured odds don't exist in forever time

a man nailed to a tree is not a good look for Easter/
let us replace him with a bunny

I learned the hard way
that
some who give the loudest applause
are
secretly planning your downfall

with the body torn in two the soul goes as one

knowledge without wisdom is just stupid

always striving to be equal and forcing it over and over seems to
reveal that you are not
believing you're equal and
living it out is more

everybody is somewhere

with every choice we make we recreate ourselves for the better or
worse

what is this excessive need to constantly promote the me?

if eternity starts today
tell me
how old are you
now

emotions can't be the gauge or moral compass that guides us

if human rights can't be defended during times of ex-
treme
then really-----------what good are they!?

how many of those who despised God
with too much reason and logic
could have lived just one more day
and possibly came to love
God
in
silence

"up"
___

crawling up from the basement
after all these years
experience has taught me plenty
biggest lesson i learned
all that i don't know
my youth spent
grinding my teeth
to the bone
the acid that
ate the stomach

crawling
up
from the basement
i catch a splinter
of the first floor light
still
quiet
serene
peaceful glow
like that
i've never known before

there must be more
there has to be more
as i struggle on four
up
those old wooden
creaking- splintered- stairs

this figure of flesh
that i caravan
is dusty
musty with the
smell of antiques
someone long ago

designed
then wore
this concrete
casket skin
that someone
knows all the
ins and outs
of
what's within
i'm learning
to love poverty
as i make my way
up
never realizing
everything gold
comes with it
all those old treasures
i stored away for preservation

no longer do i want to
sterilize myself
death is coming –
its fine-
i believe
passover
is on my side

spring cleaning
is here
i hear the
robins
tweet

out of this cellar
out of this basement floor
i hope to walk someday

utopias dream people

utopias dream people
deny deaths nail
with jubilant grin
and
world clenched in
a vaulted fist
egypt's wind -dog star orion
heaven's mystery
slams shut
syllabic light
shadowed out
closed tight
like the covers
of a once read book
shelved in humanities
literary nook

utopia's dream people
breathing within four walls
east- west- north-south
all staked out

crucify
freedom flag
into
the dying earth

this moment
this now
is our hollowed

tomorrow won't arrive
sing utopias psych science

oh
but it does
a dust storm comes
rips flesh off the bone
blackens the sun
the
almighty thumb
seals an eclipse
over the eye

we die
we die
sigh
utopia's dream people

who's
cast shadow
arrives
whose
face passes
over
these
flesh eating bacteria
under the mound
of your flag pierced
grave
when
earths shovel
dumps death
on
your
selfish utopia

without you

without you
creation has no meaning
sun set
moon rise
just motion
dead physics
measuring time

alienated
in a forest of humanity
grass grows high
over
the corpse that lies
below

feet that walked
the earth
leave footprints
no more

the moth dissolves
into invisible space
as it rockets
into the flame

drug
up the days
paralyze
the night
numb the way
that leads to light

sliding
you to the side
meaningless movement
zombie faith
activated flesh
microbial death

without you
dirt is disease
that dries to dust
flutters
away
with
the
autumnal breeze

"fall song"
_____

flowers by the side of the road
they are dying
birds
above in rows
they are flying
the grass below our feet is
browning
ol' jack o' lantern
with his crooked teeth
he is frowning

winter is coming soon
you can see it
in the face of the moon
come close hold me dear
keep me warm
throughout the year

the days
they fall so very short
the darkness
a shadow covers
your soul
the trees tossing their clothes
are shivering
while the crow's caw
through the morning

winter is coming soon
you can see it
in the face of the moon

come close hold me dear
keep me warm
throughout the year

keep me warm
through the years to come
keep me warm
I need you to hold
you're a fire
in a world
so cold

the wind is wicked in the woods
clouds hunch over
to take a look
the squirrels close their eyes
and hope through it all
while the colored leaves
wildly
F
A
L
L

* Musical Versions of this poem can befound at
https://youtu.be/1leRoCz_aFk

about the author

Dennis Jude Patronik is an American born singer/songwriter poet. He was more active performing live in the late 80s and early 90s. He enjoys all kinds of music from folk to progressive rock and is inspired by many poets, especially Dylan Thomas and Carl Sandberg. He studied religion and science and earned a degree in registered nursing and prefers a quiet life of music and writing and doesn't pursue much of a public performance lifestyle due to personal reasons. He presently resides in Buffalo, New York and is married with one son.

www.ingramcontent.com/pod-product-compliance
Lightning Source LLC
LaVergne TN
LVHW052004060526
838201LV00059B/3823